THE ROAD HOME

IMAGES OF THE OTTAWA VALLEY

*Photographs by **Steve Evans***
*Essays by **Roy MacGregor***

Published by

GENERAL STORE
PUBLISHING HOUSE INC.

1 Main Street, Burnstown, Ontario, Canada K0J 1G0
Telephone (613) 432-7697 or (613) 432-9385

ISBN 0-919431-60-7
Printed and bound in Canada

Designed by Bill Slavin, Esperança Melo and Leanne Enright

Copyright© 1992
The General Store Publishing House Inc.
Burnstown, Ontario, Canada

Canadian Cataloguing in Publication Data

Evans, Steve, 1955-
The road home: images of the Ottawa Valley

ISBN 0-919431-60-7

1. Ottawa River Valley (Quebec and Ontario)-Pictorial works.
I. MacGregor, Roy, 1948-. II. Title.

FC2775.E86 1992 917.13'8 C92-090685-0 F1054.09E93 1992

First Printing November 1992

FOREWORD

This was not our idea. It was the inspiration of Tim Gordon of the General Store Publishing House, who has probably done more to spread the secrets of the Ottawa Valley than anyone in our time. He took a photographer whose work he had published and a writer whose work he had read and decided to introduce them and see what would happen. As it turned out, we already knew — and thank God admired — each other through our work and got along famously once we'd met. A year later, after a hundred phone calls, a dozen meetings in homes and even hockey rinks, *The Road Home* is the result of Tim Gordon's hunch. For that, we are most grateful.

We are also indebted to those Tim lined up to work on this project. Bill Slavin and Esperança Melo did the design and brought it all together, selecting the photographs, the type face, the order of presentation, and, most importantly, getting it all done in time. They were assisted by another marvelous talent, Leanne Enright. Spelling and grammar mistakes were caught by the capable John Stevens and ignorance and stupidity by our irreplaceable proof-reader, Pat Bolger. Steve's muse, good luck and the weather had editing responsibility over the photographs he took. Kerry MacGregor did an extraordinary job of researching Ottawa Valley lore around her high school timetable, and we are grateful for her assistance and delighted that, in digging, she discovered herself to be as much in love with this valley as the rest of us are.

Steve Evans
Roy MacGregor

Burnstown
October 2, 1992

PASSING THROUGH

NO ONE HAS EVER SEEN ME DO THIS. Nor have I ever discussed this odd little secret with anyone — perhaps because it has no importance to anyone else but me and would sound silly said out loud, look foolish even written down on paper. But this is what I do, and have done for four decades, as I begin the long drop from the heart of Algonquin Park into the soul of the Ottawa Valley: I stare up at a brown porcelain insulator that links a telephone pole on one side of Highway 60 to a telephone pole on the other side — and I wink.

It is a wink of understanding between who I am and where I come from, a wink between the uncertain present and the certain past. I began doing this little trick as a child sitting in the back seat of the green Dodge that belonged to Tom McCormick, who was both my grandfather and Chief Ranger of Algonquin Park, and though he is 30 years dead when now I pass this point in the road he himself blazed through the Park in the 1930s, I can see the mole on the back of his neck as plain today as it was a lifetime ago. I can smell the quartered lemon my grandmother carries on a Kleenex on her lap, each wedge squeezing a little freshness, a pinch of youth onto her face as she absent-mindedly works it over her cheeks and chin while her husband drives in silence, speaking only when there is something worth mentioning, like a deer at the side of the road, or a snapping turtle on it, or a whiskeyjack over it. I can feel the cloth of their seat where my chin rests in the days before seatbelts, the days before there was any cause to protect yourself from anything.

I have no idea why I fixed on this ridiculous insulator. It lacks the magic of C.S. Lewis' closet, does not offer the mystery of Alice's mirror, but it is, for me, a link between different worlds and different times, a passage, if you will, to who I am. I have winked at it from the back seat of cars driven by grandparents and parents, from the front seat of a bewildering number of cars and trucks driven by myself. I have marked its overhead passing as a hitch-hiker and from a motorcycle. I have grown hair and lost hair while passing beneath it. I have lost grandparents and gained children. I have, so far as memory will take me back, never once missed looking up, though the winking came along much later, long after I had stopped expecting everything to make sense.

Perhaps the habit lies in the increasing truth that the insulator is the one constant in my life, the one certainty that has always been there and may be there forever, a demarcation line between a life that moves too quickly and the spread of the Ottawa Valley, where time is rendered meaningless, where no one even knows where the boundaries begin or end — and no one much cares.

To the north of this point in the road sits Source Lake. A few miles further east and you cross the Little Madawaska River, which makes a sound in spring, slows with weed in summer and is silent and unnoticed in winter. The Madawaska grows as it travels through Tanamakoon and Cache Lake and into Lake of Two Rivers, where the old ranger built his log house, where my mother, who was born in the Park, met my father, who worked in the lumber mill on the far side. It flows through Whitefish Lake and Rock Lake and Galeairy Lake where the tiny village of Whitney stands and where I was born, and from there it flows more than 100 miles through the song of the Ottawa

Valley map — Bark Lake, Kamaniskeg Bay, Hyde's Bay, Negeek, Calabogie — until at Arnprior it falls into the Ottawa River and, still spreading, flows south and east through Ottawa, where I now live.

The drive along Highway 60 to Highway 17, which brings you into Ottawa, is one of the extraordinary drives in Canada, one that ranks with the run between Jasper and Banff, the circle of Cape Breton Island and the journey North of Superior — but I see very little of the scenery as I pass beneath the insulator and begin my descent into memory. At Whitney, which is generally conceded to be the western edge of this undefineable valley, the jackpine has grown in the fine sand where the eastern gate to the Park once stood, but when I pass I do not see trees but old Mr. Cheeseman, his ranger hat perched far back on his head, raising one hand in recognition as the other pushes the ingenious weight that lifts the gate for those who belong. Sometimes I wave the way my grandfather would and I think of the lines from Tom Devine's poem about the "Opeongo Line":

On the Opeongo Line I drove a span of bays
One summer, once upon a time,
* for Hooligan and Hayes...*
Now that the bays are dead and gone
* and grim old age is mine*
A phantom team and teamster
* start from Renfrew, rain or shine...*
Aye, dreaming, dreaming,
I go teaming on the Opeongo Line.

8

Yes, phantoms, and it must be said that on the long ride through the Madawaska and Ottawa Valley, they travel well.

If you come from the Ottawa Valley, you come from another time, no matter what your personal dates. If you come to the Ottawa Valley, you enter another time, no matter what the calendar argues. Up that gravel road to the right just as Highway 60 begins heading into Whitney is Airy, which is a lovely community name for the five houses that were there when we were. In 1950 there was no electricity, no running water. The well was a quarter mile away down a steep hill. On the other side of the hill the pigs took care of the garbage. There was no telephone, certainly no television, not even a radio. The heat came from a wood stove, the wood from a shed where the slabs had to be sawn to fit. Here my mother, Helen, had the first three of her children and took care of a fourth for an ill sister-in-law. At one point she had three in diapers, including myself, no help from anyone and a husband whose job kept him six days a week in the bush. She is the strongest person I have ever known.

This situation is not described to arouse pity; quite the opposite, we felt among the privileged and were, my father working for his brother-in-law, who owned the mill. The point being made here is not to show how unusual it was to live this way into the 1950s, but how absolutely typical it was for the Ottawa Valley. In pockets, it remains so today, and it is this struggle that depicts the Valley as much as it is the white pines, the rock cuts, the music, the pink flesh of the lake trout, and the rising, invisible Valley question mark at the end of the spoken statement.

A dozen or more times a year we pass through Whitney and every time, without failure, I point out to four children where the tiny Red Cross station stood on the banks of the Madawaska and I was born. They are completely indifferent. I wish I could show them the swallows' nests that were below the foundationless houses in Airy. I wish I could point out the hideous, filthy shack where old Billy grew old and died. I wish I could show them the railway tracks where the old Ottawa, Arnprior and Parry Sound line once ran. I wish they could have seen what it was like when the last of the lumber barons, J.S.L. McRae, died and some of the pallbearers — retired men from the mill all, only a few of them owning jackets — wept as they carried him out to the black car that swept down the hill from the church and out onto Highway 60, most of the village gathered along both sides of the road as if the king had died and God alone knew what would happen next. I have no idea what they would make of such memories, but I have to believe they would make something — and if not today, then sometime when life sends everyone back along the line from which they came.

It seems foolish to suggest one could be related to road, but what else describes such intensity, such history? This same hill leading out of Whitney I have travelled in the back of the old ranger's Dodge, the warm night air cupping in off his hand and his Lands & Forests watch as we head out for Maynooth or Combermere for a night of bingo. Over this hill we would once turn off into Hay Lake where, for years, the McRae mill stood and where we would play with black labs and throw stones in the hot pond where they loosened up the bark and where we could still smell the diesel that ran the old logging alligator down by the boathouse. Over this hill we once hunted partridge, my older and younger brother and our father, and somewhere near the ghost village of Sabine on a rainy Thanksgiving weekend we came across, and photographed, a hand-written sign: "Privet — Keep Out!"

Private, yes, but come on in. The Highway bleeding off the main road south is 127 and it passes by Lake St. Peter, where another mill once stood and where the twin delights of a youngster were poking sticks at the pigs penned just the other side of the creek and a millworker named Dominic who kept an endless supply of Coffee Crisp chocolate bars for young visitors. Dominic was killed when he slipped on the gravel on his motorcycle and struck his head, and the youngster who is now a man has never eaten a Coffee Crisp since.

Around the next turn in Highway 60 is "The Growing Hills," an optical illusion as sweet as New Brunswick's Magnetic Hill but marked by neither sign nor souvenir stand nor postcard. Like most of the treasures of the Ottawa Valley it is passed down through generations. I watched the coming hill shrink and the slope we had just gone down grow from the back seat of the Dodge; my children mark it long past the age in which they truly believed it was happening; they are under oath to pass it on to theirs.

Off to the left runs l'Amable Creek and, for those who know where to look through the dancing poplars, a falls that washes over rounded granite as smooth and clear and thick as Italian crystal before exploding off the next rocks into whitewater and foam. It was not far from here in another lifetime my father brought me to fish for speckles with a huge family of Algonkin Indians, and the memory of that day — tea boiling in a tin pot over a fire, a shore lunch of speckled trout and thick butter and fresh bread, the man who pulled out a knife, waded into the alders and came back with a fishing rod so perfect I have never seen its match in the finest stores — is as rich and cherished as any along this familiar highway.

I wish I had the power to transmit the taste of chip wagon fries so drenched in vinegar the bottom of the box gives. I wish I could show you how carefully they pile the pulp wood that is hauled to the sides of this road in winter. I wish everyone could feel their hands flinch on the steering wheel when a moose suddenly rises from the near ditch, and the way every muscle in the body seems to collapse when the danger has passed and the road goes on. I wish we did not have to acknowledge that all is not postcards along such a road, that there are turns where cars have slammed into exquisite rock cuts and the Valley has lost more young people than seems fair by any measure, their blood as startling and temporary as the colors of the maple hills in fall. Too many who survive the poverty, the elements, the reckless abandon of youth, leave later anyway, for that, too, is part of being from the Valley. But those who can return, do so when they can, and think of it when they cannot. And for places like the Valley — treasured but offering no treasure — this is enough. It has to be enough.

At one time or another I have been able to claim relatives in every crossroads from Source Lake to Ottawa. Grandparents and aunts and uncles and cousins in Whitney, an uncle's family on a poor farm where the turkeys terrorized visiting children in Madawaska, someone in Barry's Bay, Killaloe, Golden Lake, Eganville, Douglas, Renfrew, Arnprior... I tell people we went to a dentist in Barry's Bay who refused to use freezing and who worked his drill with a foot treadle, but they do not believe me and sometimes I wonder if it ever did happen that way. But then I remember there is enough Valley Irish in me that it doesn't much matter how it happened; only how it's told.

❧ ❧ ❧

The view from the top of Wilno Hill is the best Ontario has to offer. It is easy to imagine the Kashubian Poles who first came here in the early 1860s looking back along the Opeongo Line, back over Round Lake and Golden Lake and the blur of the distant Black Donald Hills and realizing, for once, no one was chasing them, no one was changing their borders, denying their language, burning their books or deciding their nationality. Here they would stay and here they would farm, because farming is what they had known, even if the land seemed more suited to mountain goats than cattle and the soil was often as thin as skin over a skull and acidic from the pine rot and drip.

But here is also where you come if you wish to understand how roots can break through solid stone and sink firm in tamarack swamp. Here in the church the Kashubs put up with their own hands you can stare at the Black Madonna, the dark portrait of Our Lady of Czestochowa. The painting is a replica of the 600-year-old icon that hangs still in the Jasna Gora basilica in Poland, her face twice slashed by a maurauding Swede in the year 1665 before, legend has it, the attacker fell instantly dead on the spot. Here, in a small cathedral carved into the side of the hill, the ashes of Auschwitz dead are kept. Here along one wall, are the peach-fuzz faces of the young men who went back to Europe from Wilno a half century ago and gave their lives for their parent's new country, for the freedom their grandparents believed they might never find.

Here, on an early September day when the light is so clear you can see for 40 miles and the annual church supper is on, you can feel the roots for yourself. You can be visitor or family, and you can hope for space in a church parking lot that fills early with farmers' trucks and loggers' trucks and old cars carrying more children than seatbelts. You can be hungry, and you can line up as many times as you wish for potatoes boiled by the bag in the cauldrons out back over the open pit or the lemon meringue pie that melts in your mouth. And here you will understand that once this people had a word for getting lucky and making a deal and striking it rich and the word was *kanada*.

The drop from Wilno Hill is like a roller coaster, the blood falling from the brain, rising again, and falling again. Perhaps it is because I am always light-headed at this point that I think of Aunt Minnie and Irish wakes and strange women howling into the night. Here along the Tramore Road that runs rough along the shore of the Bonnechere River and off toward Round Lake Centre, Aunt Minnie kept a small farm that produced fresh eggs every day and fresh stones every spring.

❦ ❦ ❦

Her wake is one of my first memories, most assuredly the sharpest, and it is impossible to pass over the Bonnechere where it sweeps out into Golden Lake without thinking of the day my parents could not find someone to keep me

and so brought me along to bury Aunt Minnie.

She lay, of course, in the drawing room, a woman into her nineties in a plain casket while three women in shrouds sat nearby keening. I don't think they took her out through the window but it feels in retrospect that this is what they did. I know for certain they carried her up the gravel road to the little cemetery and used ropes to drop her and I can still hear the rap and the rattle and the heavy sliding sound the gravel made when the men gathered around the grave with spades and took turns filling it in.

This was not only a first introduction to death — a matter that seems to weigh rather more heavily in the Ottawa Valley than other places, where dying is an inconvenience rather than an event — but it was where I first encountered the blindness by agreement that runs through Valley society and can only be explained by the coming together of Irish and Scotch and French and Polish and German and Orange and Catholic: the unique genetic code of a people unto their own. This blindness concerned hard liquor, which is as relevant to the story of this world as is the white pine and the river passages and the hardship. Hard liquor and tea.

As a child at Aunt Minnie's funeral I had no place to fit. The drawing room where she lay gagged me with the smell of flowers. The women taking turns keening were terrifying. One woman grabbed me and lifted me up and forced me to touch Aunt Minnie so I would never be afraid of the dead. I escaped to the kitchen and the sitting room where the clatter of tea cups and loud talk was drowning out the keening, but there were more women than seats in the house and no room to move. The smell of lilac water and powder was as suffocating as the flowers in the death room. A handful of date squares and I headed outside intending to play with the chickens and drop stones down the well — but instead I learned one of the most vital lessons of Valley life: wherever men gather, pumps break down. Or wood needs cutting. Or carburetors need their idle set.

In Aunt Minnie's case, there being no car on the farm or pump in the basement — no basement, for that matter — the men were cutting wood. At least that is how the women would describe it if asked. And the men, as well, but with flushed grins. Out in Aunt Minnie's woodshed they were slamming back the rye, straight and straight out of three or four small bottles they passed back and forth as they stood in the circle and talked about everything but what was going on this day:

"...McRae's'll draw more'n 100 million feet this year..."

"...You won't see much partridge this fall. Summer's been too wet, eh?..."

"...No goddam use even thinkin' lake trout in August — they're down too deep..."

This, I would learn over many years, is the way drinking was done in the Ottawa Valley — and to an extent still is. Women and men gather for a funeral or a wedding or just as family and when the kettle is coming to a boil for tea, the men are called off to fix the pump or cut some wood or stare into a car hood. Here is where the drinking is done, hard and fast, and everyone, the women and the men, pretends nothing was ever served but tea and coffee. The men get *tight*, not drunk, but the subject of drink is never raised unless one of the men gets "drunk", not tight — and then the blindness by agreement is set aside and a scene is allowed if the woman concerned wishes to create one. It is a bizarre ritual that has never made sense but has more lasting power than would seem possible. And some of the forms it can take on are nothing short of ridiculous.

There are satellites that can detect certain metals in the ground; if there were one that could detect buried booze the space map would light up like a Christmas tree as the satellite passed over the Ottawa Valley. I have been driving with my father when, on a lonely stretch of road in the middle of the bush, he has pulled over, removed a shovel and a burlap sack from the trunk, walked off toward a culvert where water trickles through into peat and muskeg and returned with the sack full of cold beer. My brother has been miles back in the bush, moving through a canoe portage when one of his companions came across a mickey of brandy when he moved a pile of rocks for other reasons — and later, when telling the story, he has had an old uncle shout, "Goddam it all to hell, that's *my* mickey! *I* put it there!"

Such eccentricities, combined with a dialect as unique to the Ottawa Valley as the language of Newfoundland is to the Rock, make this country an island of another type, cut off by distance and spruce, by time and money, by tradition and terrain, Algonquin Park blocking the West, the North petering out into itself, the Ottawa River and the rock-faced Gatineau Hills preventing any spread east and the suburban sprawl of those who came from elsewhere forming a fence to the south and east where the city begins and the Valley ceases, at least psychologically.

It is not unfair to say much of the Ottawa Valley exists in our heads. Most of the people of the Valley have left and return only in good weather and at Christmas; their Valley is in the head, and often more beautiful and always warmer and certainly simpler than it is for those who have stayed on or those who decided, even at great sacrifice, to come and stay on.

❧ ❧ ❧

As the road passes through Golden Lake, it touches on the Golden Lake reserve of the Algonkin Indians, and while I have been fortunate enough to write extensively about, and travel extensively within, the native communities of this country, I can never know what it is like to have been born in Golden

Lake and to have grown up here. Some wonderful; some terrible. Those who have are filled with love for the air and for family and for the clear gilt-flecked water. They are filled, as well, with a growing sense of past injustices, wrongs which current governments are only now coming to terms with as the huge Algonkin land claim — which includes land from Parliament Hill to Algonquin Park — heads toward some unknown resolution, the only certain outcome that it will deeply rile those who believe the inequities must not be changed in either direction.

At Eganville the water is hard and tastes like iron. Here I had my first real barber shop haircut. Here I discovered that the most marvelous experience in the world was to stand in the bakery line at Lisk's when the cinnamon rolls came out of the oven. Here I learned, much to my astonishment, that there were creatures called domestic raspberries as large as thimbles and sweeter, but somehow not as good, as the wild ones that grew along the hydro lines to the east of Whitney.

Here in Eganville is where my father was born in 1907 and where my mother was sent for high school, and the stories here are too many to tell. My father, whose own father died when my father was but four years old, grew up here. I have a faded photograph of the 1927-28 Eganville Senior Hockey Team and he is standing third from the right with his hair split down the middle as straight as a plumb line. I have heard him talk of playing along the river then, of heading out in cutters and covered in buffalo blankets to play the Douglas team in matches that brought out both communities. I have laughed every time he tells the story of the referee who blew the play down in the middle of the game, then skated slowly to the bank, peed with his back to the crowd and then returned to centre ice for the face-off.

Beyond Eganville lies the choice of three routes heading toward the Ottawa River. Highway 60 runs through Douglas, the majestic Catholic Church and cemetery on the left, the poor Protestants buried on the right. There was once a grist mill here and once it was owned by a distant relative, but now there are only the footings and broken concrete. If you choose not to go through Douglas you must turn down the Barr Line, which runs by the cheese factory, where once you could stand and watch them skim the whey. The quickest route empties onto Highway 17 at Cobden, where local legend has it that a monster once hid in Muskrat Lake and where recent history has it that a man spent a fortune trying, unsuccessfully, to bring it to the surface. Somehow, it is difficult not to think if this mystery is ever solved it will not be in Loch Ness or the Okanagan Valley of British Columbia, but right here where French flair and Polish superstitition and Irish exaggeration came a century ago and put a monster in the water for fun even if one was never there in fact.

At Renfrew the Bonnechere flows beneath the road and heads for the Ottawa, the river beginning to widen. At Arnprior the Madawaska — now wide itself, hopelessly distanced from the Little Madawaska that trickled near Source Lake — moves from granite into shale and merges with the Ottawa, still widening.

It was near Cobden where they found the old astrolabe in the ground and put up a very Irish plaque claiming it had been Champlain's own, that he had used it to measure the stars that guided him down the St. Lawrence and up the Ottawa. An instrument of such uncanny accuracy in the hands of a man who believed he was on his way "to the Kingdom of China and the East Indies."

If only Champlain could have known. It was not China he was heading for, but Pembroke. And where he would drop his sextant they would one day rebuild Noah's Ark and put up a sign claiming a water slide second to none known on heaven or earth.

China, he thought. But it was the Ottawa Valley — and for those who know where to look, as exotic as any place still open these days to ambitious explorers.

15

Window on the Opeongo Line, Barry's Bay.

17

Bill Dodge's General Store, Calabogie.

18

Supplies and service, Elphin Gas Station.

19

Roadside eye-catcher. Village of Lanark.

Getz General Store, a Killaloe Station landmark.

Formal entry to Golden Lake coin laundry.

Texture and contrast, the Man's World Barbershop, Pembroke.

26

Stained glass church window, Lanark County.

Log homestead, Spruce Hedge.

On the French Line,
Lanark County.

Dog and church, Poland.

31

Rooflines, silver and blue, Douglas.

Collector Jim Willington, Kemptville.

South March homestead, high summer.

37

There are places in the Valley you hope will never change.
Balmoral Hotel, Barry's Bay.

38

Balmoral Hotel, Barry's Bay.

39

THE PEOPLE

"THE OTTAWA COUNTRY," RAN THE advertisement in the August 28, 1856 edition of the *St. Catharines Journal*, "...is capable of sustaining a population of eight million people." And if you want to see all eight million of them in one place, just try finding a table any Saturday night at Fred's up in Chapeau, on the north shore of the Ile des Allumettes, Quebec side of the Ottawa River — where the bars stay open long after the Valley brain has shut down for the weekend.

Come, push through the noise and smoke for a seat by the far wall, a single empty seat just under the fur-bearing lake trout that was taken from waters so cold the fish have adapted by growing better insulation than scales provide. While the waiter pushes through the neon haze with his tray of cold draft and quart bottles, a pickled egg for the old guy in the corner, I will tell you about Jack Gervais, the old Park ranger who claimed he once found a spring-fed creek — that's right,

buddy, *crick* — so cold he used to wait downstream for the speckles to pass over the source, freeze solid, and then he would stack them like cordwood along the bank.

But my stories are weak compared to Fred's. Go with him now, while he walks you through the room and explains the photographs on the wall and the stuffed animals and the artifacts. Perhaps if you are lucky and you ask Fred nicely, he will show you the rare silver beaver he has stashed in the freezer in the back. That's correct — a silver beaver. But first you must tour the walls: the rabbits with the antlers, the fish so large they fit the canoe like a German sausage on a hot dog bun, the beast that is part turtle, part frog, part muskrat, part beaver, part rabbit, part fish, part mystery...

"You ever hear of a silver beaver?" Fred asked me the first time I came here long after those with better sense had gone to bed.

"I've heard of silver fox," I said, quickly

41

establishing my bush credentials.

"Nothin' like this."

I had once, in an old Valley dump on an August evening, seen an old black bear with one silver side. I have seen a black wolf. An albino deer. A two-headed garter snake. But Fred just stood there grinning, waiting.

"You wanna see it?"

"Yah. Sure."

Go with him now and he will take you, too. It is dark in the back room and the bare bulb bleeds in the smoke that rushes in from the bar. There is light in the freezer, however, and when Fred lifts the lid you can stare down into the greatest mystery of the entire Ottawa Valley...

...a genuine silver beaver ...cold as metal.

It sometimes seems like there are too many stories to tell. My Uncle Lorne Pigeon could talk about when he was a child growing up in Madawaska, the middle of more than a dozen children, and how they would schedule two hours for the walk into church from the farm just to make sure there was enough time to get all the fights in. My brother, Jim, could tell you about the weekend we went in to the mill to pick up our father and found him, fast asleep in the empty bunkhouse, with a copy of Plutarch's Lives on his chest and a loaded .22 leaning on the wall beside him in case the wolves, having already killed his dog, came back.

Stan Darling, the 80-year-old Member of Parliament for Muskoka-Parry Sound — and, after twenty solid years of driving back to his riding every cursed weekend, most assuredly the politician who has travelled most through the Ottawa Valley — could tell of the time he ploughed his brand-new white Cadillac onto a moose calf that had run out and slipped on the pavement before he could swerve or brake, how the new car rode up over the doomed animal and how, to get him home without gagging from the smell, the boys at the Shell station in Whitney gave Stan a fistful of pine tree air fresheners to stuff up his nostrils while he himself hoofed it back to Ottawa.

The census takers have never come up with the eight million people who were supposed to settle the Valley. Nor are there quite enough hermits, squatters and tax evaders to make up the slack — though the Ottawa Valley would count more of these than most places, if counting were possible. But there are eight million stories, and counting.

Joan Finnigan, who has made a living interviewing the oldtimers of the Ottawa Valley and writing about the history, knows most of them, and more than a few involving her own father, Fearless Frank Finnigan. Old Frank became a professional hockey player at the age of thirteen when the Quebec village of Quyon slipped him ten dollars to help them have revenge on Fitzroy Harbour, straight across the river on the Ontario side. "The Shawville Express," with his two Stanley Cup rings and fourteen years of National Hockey League stardom, lived to the age of 91 and would surely be in the Hall of Fame were it not for his being too much from the Valley, too determined to take life beyond the limits, the "F. Scott Fitzgerald of the sporting world," in the poetry of his daughter.

"...I remember my father, too, in the headlines,
on the gum cards, in the rotogravure,
and how, in the pasture, there was nothing
to charge but shadows and, in the dark beyond
night,
bright enormous butterflies crossing the moon
of his disenchanted vision; I heard him cry out
to them
in another room but they stayed in his eyes
until we were all well-marked by the days
of his going down into ruin..."

Joan Finnigan could tell warm and happy stories of Fearless Frank, as well. And she could tell of other fabulous stories of strength: Joseph Montferrand, better known as "Joe Mufferaw," the Paul Bunyan of the Ottawa Valley who could leave the imprint of his calk boots on a barroom ceiling, or John Goth of Malicoff who chopped three cord of wood a day for eight years in a time when cords of wood were measured properly. She could tell stories of wealth: John Rudolph Booth, who started a shingle mill on nine dollars and eventually employed 4,000 shantymen, built his own railway through to Parry Sound, made millions, lived to be 99 and spent his final years walking around his camps looking for

horseshoes to salvage; or Harry McLean, the construction giant who began life as a waterboy, ended as a multi-millionaire, was banned from every fancy hotel in the country and yet was beloved by the commonfolk as the eccentric "Mister X" who threw away his money on the street and tossed bills out of hotel rooms when he was allowed to register. She could tell about the Laird of McNab, the Highland chief who fled financial ruin in Scotland and tried to re-create the feudal system on the outskirts of Arnprior.

If you wish, you yourself can turn such stories into more than words. There are still stone and log buildings from McNab's days along the Lower Madawaska. And high on the windswept White Lake cemetery there is a plot that lay unmarked for decades, the final resting place of the Laird's housekeeper, "Granny" Fisher, and their illegitimate son, Allan Francis, who was better known as "Allan Dhu," or "Black Allan." And if you know the right places to ask, there are still old-timers to be found who will swear that Black Allan gained his name from the rape and murder of Indian girls he set upon when they were walking alone.

Indian girls, the nameless and faceless in a history that rings too much with men and deeds and old-country names. Today, those who know where to look head back of Palmer Rapids for the log cabin that, back in the Roaring Twenties and Dirty Thirties was said to serve as Al Capone's hideaway. They can

43

find where Cyclone Taylor once played for the Renfrew Millionaires. They can pass by the over-sized lumber barons' homes in Pembroke. They can visit the clearing along the Tay River in Perth where, in 1833, the last pistol duel was fought in Canada between two young law students, Robert Lyon and John Wilson, with Lyon bleeding to death from his wound and Wilson going on to a distinguished career as an Ontario judge. They can talk to the children and grandchildren — I am myself a great-grandchild — of the Ottawa Valley shantymen and rivermen who joined General Wolseley's Nile Expedition in the winter of 1884-85 and paddled into Khartoum two days after the city had fallen and General Charles Gordon had been killed.

All men. But where are the tales of the women who, far too often alone, kept the families alive while the men headed off into the bush to earn their miserable wage — money which again too often never even made it back home with them? Where are the nurses and midwives who accomplished what there were too few doctors to do? Where are the women who cleared and burned and turned the soil and chopped the firewood and slaughtered the pigs and chinked the logs? Where were the storytellers to glorify *their* contributions? To understand why it is women make up the only the subtext of the rough and rolling history of the Ottawa Valley, it is necessary to walk slowly through the overrun graveyards filled with devil's paintbrush and

fading white tombstones, the graveyards of Round Lake Centre and Combermere and Griffith and Westmeath and Fort-Coulonge and Deux Rivieres and Lanark and Calabogie and Mount St. Patrick and Luskville and Maynooth and Burnstown — and note in particular the short, startling gap between date of birth and date of death, and all too often the number of infants buried with her.

Suffering and dying, violence and death are also part of the Valley story. What precious little earth there is that is deeper than skin over rock and thicker than sphagnum over swamp has too often been turned over to burials instead of crops. And too many of those who opened up this brutally-beautiful country ended up lost too early, the victims of tragedy and disease and hardship and the bitter, heartless elements.

"There is," wrote Charlotte Whitton in *A Hundred Years A' Felling*, "one passage on the Madawaska where, it is said that, on a clear night of the May full moon, eerie cries and haunting shouts echo. There a crib, buckling with shoals, carried its crew to death among the ragged rocks and crashing timber and to this day some swear that the spirits of the lost men shift among the mists and the trees of the shore, seeking sepulchre."

No one knows how many men died trying to work the bush, how many men and women and children died trying to survive it. The postcards of the Rideau Canal say nothing of the men who died building it, killed by quarry

44

blasts, by drowning, by disease and, in some cases — including that of Col. John By, who masterminded the construction — killed by the work itself.

To understand fully what it was like to be one of those who fled famine in Ireland to end up in the Ottawa Valley, it is advisable first to visit Grosse Ile off Quebec City where the ships were first quarantined and where, in 1832 alone, more than 1,000 died of cholera and were buried in what is still known as the Valley of Death. *"Far from their own beloved isle,"* poet Thomas O'Hagan wrote in 1909, after a visit to Grosse Ile,

> *Those Irish exiles sleep;*
> *And dream not of historic past,*
> *Nor o'er its memories weep;*
> *Down where the blue St. Lawrence tide*
> *Sweeps onward, wave on wave,*
> *They lie — old Ireland's exiled dead,*
> *In cross-crowned lonely grave."*

It is crucial to understand that so many of those who came to the Ottawa Valley were fleeing, running from a past that hadn't worked out. It is a symptom that runs true from the Irish leaving famine in the 1830s to the Poles running from enemies in the 1860s to young Americans turning their backs on politics in the 1960s. Scots, French, German — all came in search of freedom and opportunity. And it shaped them profoundly. Even the Algonkin Indians who ended up in places like Golden Lake on the Ontario side and Barriere Lake on the Quebec side were moving first from the Iroquois, who tried to drive them out of the Valley, and later from the Whites, who sought to squeeze them out.

Those who come from this land and treasure what it has given them have an extraordinary sense of unfairness. The Irish had God Himself against them. The Scots-Irish were despised by the English Anglicans, suspected by the Irish Catholics, denied public office and subjected to intolerable rent increases. The Germans had opportunity denied them, war plaguing them. The Polish had been so oppressed by belligerent, ambitious neighbors that, at one point in 1795, the nation had actually disappeared from the map of Europe.

Such inequity should have built a quick empathy between those who fled to the Valley and those who were already here when they arrived. In 1613, when the French explorer Samuel de Champlain reached what is now known as Muskrat Lake near Cobden, his party was met by Nibachis, the chief, who decided Champlain must have fallen from the clouds, there being no other possible explanation for the sudden appearance of such strange creatures. Nibachis then happily offered the Whites tobacco as a gift and invited them to carry on up the river. Two centuries later, in 1822, the Crown purchased this land Nibachis so willingly shared for a mere 65 British pounds — purchased, it is worth noting, from the Mississauga Band of Ojibwas who had never so much as seen the

Algonkin land they so willingly "surrendered."

Those who came to make up the Ottawa Valley were, one and all, outsiders and proud of it. It would be wrong to say the mix produced a perfect harmony. The Algonkin would have problems with that proposition. And White history has recorded the incident at Brennan's Creek Bridge when, during a turn of the century election, the Irish came to beat up on the Poles who'd said they wouldn't vote for an English-speaking candidate and the Poles quickly put an end to the argument with a fierce show of pitchforks. No, it was never perfect, but shared experience and past inequities did create certain characteristics common to all who come from the Valley or who came by choice to the Valley to call it home.

From the Irish and Polish came sentimentality. The Ottawa Valley holds the same grip on the displaced and over-sized heart as Newfoundland and Cape Breton, two other rough Canadian regions inhabited by the Irish and the Scotch. *"Thou barren waste; unprofitable strand,"* wrote a disenchanted Standish O'Grady when he came to Canada from Ireland in the 1830s.

Where hemlocks brood on unproductive land,
Whose frozen air on one bleak winter's night
Can metamorphose dark brown hares to white!
Here forests crowd, unprofitable lumber,
O'er fruitless lands indefinite as number.

But it was a minority opinion. " We are new men in a new country," wrote Thomas

D'Arcy McGee, who would go on to become one of the Fathers of Confederation. "Our affairs are with the Imperial Government and the American Republic, not with James II or William III." And nowhere in Canada did the displaced Irish feel more Irish than up the Opeongo Line.

Much of this vital transportation line was opened up by the Poles, beginning with sixteen families who left the German port of Bremen in 1858 and arrived eleven weeks later in Quebec City, having lost several members to typhus and hunger and a hideously rough crossing. Having left a world where their own language had been outlawed and their books burned, they soon built their own school and taught their children in Polish. Many even committed to memory the words to Zygmunt Krasinski's Przedswit that had taken an earlier generation through the blackest days when the Russians and Prussians were overrunning what had once been Poland.

"...and I heard
A voice that called in the eternal sky:
As to the world I gave a Son,
So to it, Poland, thee I give.
My only Son He was — and shall be,
But in thee my purpose for Him lives.
Be thou then the Truth, as He is, everywhere.
Thee I make my daughter!
When thou didst descend into the grave
Thou wert, like Him, a part of humankind."

If Poland meant this much, then Wilno — where the Kashubs settled in 1864 and, finally, felt safe — would mean almost as much. Here they would put up their church, here they would eventually erect the roadside plaque honoring "Canada's First Polish Settlement," and here other Poles would come from around the world to make a pilgrimage to the safe haven that once seemed like the Poland that had been wiped from the map of the world.

The Scots brought their stubbornness and emotional guards. The French brought individuality and a fervour for life. Germans brought industry. But the passage of years and genes ensured that the stereotypes could never hold, and eventually a personality indigenous to the Ottawa Valley emerged on its own. No matter whether you go to the Labor Day church supper at Wilno or head off in March to Gavan's Hotel in Quyon, where St. Patrick's Day lasts two days, there is something consistent about the people, something particular to the blend.

These are the people of the Valley. Sentimental and stubborn. Stoic Monday through Friday; Fred's late Saturday night. Defiant of authority and admiring of enterprise. Suspicious of strangers yet so trusting many doors will go unlocked into the twenty-first century. Devoted, long after the rest of North America has changed to bookings, to dropping in out of the blue on relatives and friends, a natural habit that may well have survived into the second half of this century for the simple reason that, even if one thought of phoning ahead, there was often no

phone to receive the call anyway.

And above all, language. It is the secret handshake of the Valley, the one that identifies all to one another, the trapping that sets us apart in degrees, for the strength of the Valley brogue is as good as an official *curriculum vitae* of where one was born, where one was raised and how long one has stayed. The standing joke, of course, is "Gidday, gidday," but this barely scratches the surface of the second most distinct dialect in Canada, accommodating Valley folks willing to concede to Newfoundland only so long as an asterisk is included to point out Newfoundland joined Canada in 1949, more than a century after the first Irish declared the Ottawa Valley a "corker."

It is heavily Irish, of course, but heavily affected by other influences, the most important being the Polish effect on the pronunciation of "th" — *dat* instead of *that*, *dis* instead of *this*. Here the men are all "lads," here they say "prit near" for "close" and "kooky" for "cookie" and "beyant" for "beyond" and "tarble" and "turrible" for "terrible." Here when certain men say "dang" their family and neighbors cover their ears.

You can pick up this language from Lake Capimitchigama, where the Ottawa begins, to Lac des Deux-Montagnes, where the waters flow into the St. Lawrence, from Source Lake, where the Madawaska begins, to Arnprior, where it empties. The language persists where history cannot hold: there are now more rubber rafts floating down the Ottawa River than there are logs.

But that, really, is the point. The Ottawa Valley is neither history nor geography. We know not where it began in time, only when some of us arrived and it was waiting. No one is even certain where it is found: Perth is in no valley; the Madawaska has its own peculiar geology. Hardly anyone speaks funny on Parliament Hill — though that is not to suggest they are not to be laughed at. No, the true Ottawa Valley is found on the tongue, in the heart and — all too often — in the memory of those who know exactly where they are from and where they will always call home, no matter where their forwarding address.

And it is found in the ability to laugh at oneself after the lid has gone down on the silver beaver and Fred has ushered you back into the bar where a bell is ringing and, it seems, eight million people from the Valley are pointing and laughing, laughing, laughing...

Tradition carried on. The twelfth of July Orangemen's Parade, Richmond.

King Billy, Orangemen's Parade, Lanark.

52

Orangemen marching with banners, Richmond.

53

Following the flag of freedom, twelfth of July, Richmond.

Volunteers clean the Catholic church, Wilno.

Attending to details, Wilno.

57

Time stands still. Orville Corell and John Sinnott, Lombardy.

58

Open expanses. Ken Evans, Pakenham.

59

Roy Brown, scarecrow artist, with his work,
North Augusta.

Clifford Le Brun, of a long line of loggers, Arnprior.

62

The lumber trade persists in the Valley. James Wojcik, Madawaska.

Mrs. Crosbie behind the counter, Flower Station.

64

An old-fashioned general store. Martin and Pat Lynch, Douglas.

65

Ernie Smith training his trick horse.
Fitzroy Harbour.

66

Hubert Huyer, Springtown.

67

Kevin and Mary McHugh, Spruce Hedge.

68

Kevin McHugh with his cows, Spruce Hedge.

Anna Whiteduck and Dorothy Commanda,
Golden Lake Reserve.

Olive Brown, Richmond.

72

Louis Riopelle, Burnstown.

73

Eric Pordonick, lumber man, Whitney.

Three Valley lads; Gary Cannon, Edmond Kuiack, Philip Kuiack. McRae Lumber Mill, Whitney.

Looking up from the local news.
Vince Peplinskie, Killaoe.

Roy Craig, Clyde Forks.

Ken Kirkham, Perth.

81

Bill Dodge and his dog Rex, Calabogie.

Douglas "Buttons" Young, Oxford Mills.

83

Ruth Smart, Shawville.

84

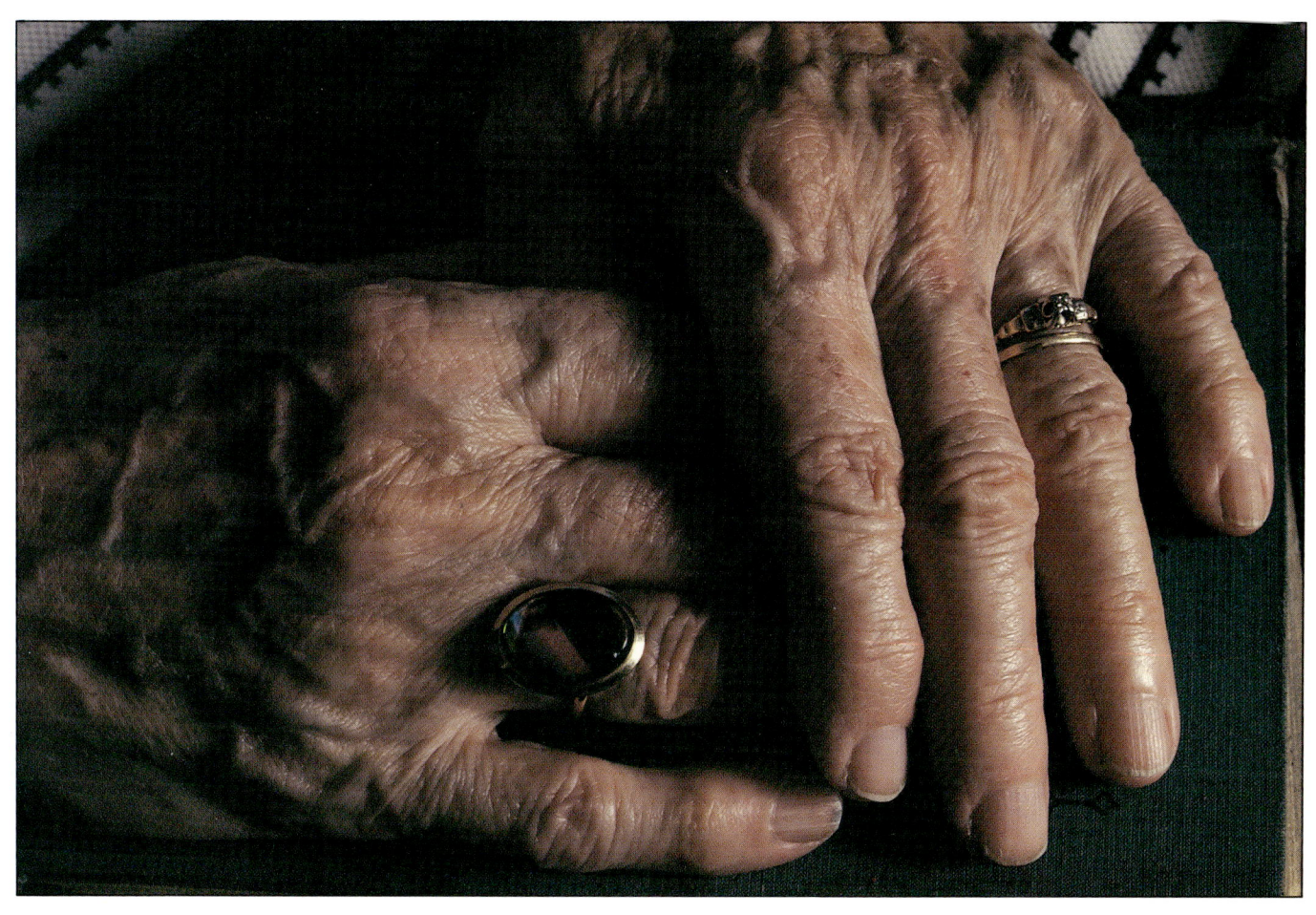

The hands of Mary Nelson, Richmond.

85

Rusty Leach, a fixture at the Chapeau Hotel, Chapeau.

Locals as film extras, Almonte.

SUMMER

IT IS NOW TWENTY YEARS SINCE EARL SHOWED ME that time doesn't run in straight lines through the Ottawa Valley. It was the first summer after Ellen and I were married, and I wanted her, with her roots in southwestern Ontario and Manitoulin Island and Saskatchewan, to see where my people had come from; and so we set off from Toronto, where we first lived, passed through Algonquin Park and drove east along Highway 60 until we dropped down a high, maple-ridged hill into the village of Eganville. Here my father had been born and raised and had, during the early 1920s, briefly operated an ice cream stand on the bridge over the Bonnechere, before admitting he had no head for business and set out instead for a life in the lumber camps. Here my mother and her three brothers and sister had gone on to high school after they had finished with the little one-room schoolhouse at Brule Lake. And here there were still relatives and family friends, and Earl.

I'm not sure how to describe Earl except to say his first name will suffice. If you need to picture him, think of a face that has never aged, of eyes as bright and clear and trusting as a child's, a small man neatly turned out in hardy cottons and denim , and a stylish straw hat somewhat stained by the sweat of his work in the extraordinary garden that was his father's pride and joy, right up until the old man's recent death — a death that Earl perhaps describes best as "Daddy fell and broke his heart." Earl is the brother of my mother's close childhood friend, the good son of a tall and very kind old man, the charge, from the moment of the old man's unfortunate passing, of a wonderful housekeeper who, over the years, had become the soul of the family itself. In other settings, Earl might have grown up in an institution. In Eganville, he grew up in Eganville.

If we go back yet another twenty years or more, Earl is much the same and I am much

91

younger, a child standing in this same proud garden as Earl, giggling with delight, picks raspberry after raspberry and drops them, ripe and juicy and big as thimbles, into the red-stained and outstretched hands of children who have never before seen domestic raspberries. To the children from Whitney, they seem a different fruit entirely from the wild ones they pick along the road shoulders and hydro line. The huge, sweet berries are as unknown and surprising as the taps and flushing toilet they encountered when their parents took them to the nearest large town for eye checkups, booked them all into a motel room while the parents made the appointments and returned to find a flooded room and a furious manager. Earl watches us when we visit. He makes sure no one steps on the cucumber, takes us to the river to swim and waits in the shade of his straw hat for us to tire, then takes us back up the hill to the old house. As far as he is concerned, nothing ever changes. And as he says to me moments after meeting my wife, "You and me is pals still."

Absolutely. And as we walk through the garden and around the house, Earl reminds one who is starting to take the world and himself too seriously that there are other ways of looking at life. Earl, for example, says he can still see his father standing on the porch, calling for him. He can hear him speak. And he has committed to memory the last words the old man said when he lay in his deathbed after falling and breaking his heart. "He said

I was the best son a man ever had." This is not said with sorrow, but pride. And it is also pride that rings through when Earl says the garden is as good this year as any year.

"We'll leave the women here yakking and go off for some exploring," Earl says.

There is nothing to discuss. He is already in the car, a small man in the front seat, hat slipped back over the tan line, smiling as his beloved village, his home, begins to unfold over the windshield. We pass a wedding car and, giggling, he leans over to honk the horn. We pass a man walking back from the bakery who stops and stares, and then a woman who glances up from her chair in the shade of a dusty elm.

"I'll bet they're wondering where them guys is off to, eh?" Earl says.

Perhaps. Perhaps they know, for in the Ottawa Valley, visitors go for drives less to see what has changed than to see again what remains the same.

❧ ❧ ❧

They return in summer, when the Valley looks its best. It is the season of the Ottawa Valley for it is summer when they come back home, summer when they find the time and the need to touch again their own memories and the record of those who went before them, summer when those who live here all the time are most proud of that fact and certain of its rightness. There is Christmas, but it is hurried and overly-scheduled and sometimes missed.

92

There are no family reunions in November. There are few motel rooms available in March, and it is not because of heavy bookings. Only because there is just no use.

That is not to say winter in the Valley has no appeal of its own. On days when the snow does not lasso over the highway and the wind stab from the north, winter can offer a sharpness so bright the valley can seem like the cleanest, finest, freshest place on earth. When the lakes and rivers are frozen and someone has cleared off a rink and the children have come down with their skates and sticks and someone has cut a hole for drinking and someone else is building a fire, the Valley is as sweet and simple as this complicated country ever gets. When the Northern Lights spread across the wide fields north of Cobden heading into Pembroke and on toward Deep River, a night trip can feel like the gates of heaven have opened and you are simply driving through for a curiosity gawk the way you might drive past the better cottages along the river on a summer evening.

Nor is any of this said to slight fall, when the calendars and postcards show their interest in the Ottawa Valley. Coming into Madawaska, the hills on one side are feather yellow with birch and poplar, on the other, fire truck red with sugar maple. Back of Brudenell the tamarack turns so rusty soft it seems they could make beds of the swamp trees now that the mosquitoes are gone. All down through the river corridor the sky above

the escarpment is checkmarked with Canadian geese, their sound from a distance like children playing. In the distance — not always far enough — shots are heard, shotguns muffled, rifles cracking. The water is black now, having turned. The air sometimes carries the scent of burning leaves, the smell of all childhoods but for the more recent, deprived ones under suburban bylaws. But it also rains too much, cold and slanting rain that hurts the cheek and squeezes the heart. Fall means the year is over and done, and they will not return until well after the geese themselves have passed back overhead.

Spring in the Ottawa Valley lasts about five hours, and there is nothing to say about it apart from the fact that it was here sometime yesterday and we are now well into summer — even though there is still snow in the bush.

No, summer is how we see the Valley when we are not there and we find ourselves thinking about it. All past memory is dated summer. All glorious descriptions we pass on to those who have never been there are summer descriptions. All longing is for summer, no matter what the season or where we are when we pine for the Ottawa Valley. It is always summer in our heads.

❧ ❧ ❧

Earl and I head down the gravel backroads, his straw hat bobbing as he talks a million words a minute. A partridge, stupid with summer, stands to the side of the road and does not move even though we stop, and the sight of the partridge — no one in the valley ever says "ruffed grouse" — sends Earl off on a reminiscence that may or may not be true. It simply does not matter. In his memory there are "little deers tippy-toeing" and groundhogs standing on bales of hay and a smart old fox slipping away into the grass. And since I can see it all clearly as he speaks, it is true enough, for if it didn't actually happen in our past it has happened in our conversation, our shared memory, and for those who come from people and land where the past is a high art, the remembering takes legal precedent over the happening.

My own memories of summer are also suspect, but also excused. Each summer now that I am grown older, I make sure our four children spend a day on that magnificent southern-exposure point where the old ranger built his two-storey log home, tacked on a porch and signed, like the great artist he indeed was, the last board of trim he nailed up: "Thomas I. McCormick, Sept. 10, 1940." We dive off the high rocks and I explain that the water passing by will flow through the Madawaska system and into the Ottawa and eventually pass by the town in which they now live. I show them where the house stood and where my mother and I once sifted through the rubble left by the bulldozer that came in and razed the foundation and where we found that final, signed board of trim and his old shaving mug, not a chip in it. I show them

where the flag was raised each morning and lowered each evening and I tell them how upset the old ranger would become if the flag were not folded properly or it should touch the ground. I show them the pier he built in front of the summer kitchen one spring when the water was so high there was fear it would float away. I show them where the ice house stood, where the fireplace was, where my brothers and sister played. And I pretend not to notice when they roll their eyes at me and move on to the next lecture in what it was like when it was right.

But how I wish they could share those moments, even those which may only have happened in my head. I wish they, who complain about the lack of air conditioning in the van that brings them here, could know what it is like to cool one's arms on a hot summer's day by plunging them fist first into the flour bin that once was in the kitchen that is here no more. I wish they could feel what it is like to squiggle one's toes deep into the wet, cold sawdust that kept the ice, and what it is to run from the ice house with sawdust stockings and how the wood will dry and flake off and tickle as it goes.

I wish I could somehow teach them the lessons that came to me by accident. The day my older brother, Jim, found twenty-three dollars floating in the lake — a huge sum in the mid-1950s, a complete mystery as to how the bills came to be lying around the near bay — and how the old ranger took him in to the

94

Whitney detachment of the Ontario Provincial Police so the money could be turned in as lost, and how 60 days later the police called to say no one had claimed the money and my brother then had the first pair of new hockey skates any of us had ever owned. I wish they could travel with me and the old ranger that morning when the call came in from headquarters that there had been an "incident" at the dump — a little girl had tried to feed her cream soda to a cub and the mother bear had cuffed her away — and the rangers had been forced to take action. Off we went to investigate, and I have never forgotten the old man's expression when he arrived to see the rangers sitting quietly, like mourners at a lying-in, while around them seven bears lay dead, including the mother and her cub with the fatal sweet tooth.

But how I wish they could come back with me for a walk through those times. I wish they could stand on the side of the road and wait for the big green cab of Brooks' Transport to rise from the heat ripples over the curve on the hill, and then for a nickle buy a popsicle from the driver, ice cold from the little freezer, soon dripping orange across your knuckles in the sun. I wish they could come again to the Red Cross picnic in Whitney and feel what children then felt when they were handed that bent coathanger and reached with it over the army blanket strung across the doorway and feel the jiggle as cousin Marjorie checked first through a tear in the blanket to see who was fishing

and then attached a suitable toy. I wish they could be there, for those things that did happen as well as those that might have happened.

"Do you think we should be getting back?" Earl asks.

As much as possible, yes.

❧ ❧ ❧

There is something about the Canadian summer. So transitory, so fleeting. Some of us begin to panic the moment the days turn shorter, panic that the country's most valued currency is passing through our hands and we have not spent it wisely. Summer, after all, is our secret time, the few weeks when we believe we are our truest selves. It begins with sparklers on Victoria Day weekend, ends in embers on Thanksgiving. By then the seasons have reversed. Leaves no longer shade, but reveal. Relief is found inside rather than outside, in fire rather than water. On certain October mornings, the lake steams.

Summer in the Ottawa Valley is when you stand by a chip wagon late in the evening and care less when you are served. It is enough breeze to keep away the mosquitoes. It is when you wade out so far in Golden Lake it seems you will never have the depth to swim. It is red trim on Round Lake, mirrored calm on the river north of Pembroke, water falling from a hand pump in Mount St. Patrick. It is deer flies around the ankles and a canoe wobbling. It is a snapping turtle groggy in the sun. It is a

95

child collecting toads while his parents pick enough berries for a pie.

In summer it is possible to tell time by the ripenings. Summer begins with wild strawberries hiding in the grass on sandy knolls, moves into raspberry and blueberry and begins to fade with chokecherry.

There are people here who can walk through the woods the way a computer searches through a data base. They know when the pin cherry flowers. They can point out marsh marigold, baneberry, lamb's quarters, wild cucumber and swamp candles. They know which fern to pick early for fiddleheads. They know when the sumac is the color of fire. And there are those, as well, who simply enjoy a walk through the woods without proper names, but who recognize the Ottawa Valley at its best all the same.

❧ ❧ ❧

I cannot reproduce for my children the summers as they were. In all likelihood they were not even as remembered. But I can tell them what it was like to walk out to the edge of Highway 60 where the car was parked and to sit long into the night while my father and brother pulled in baseball games from New York and Detroit and Chicago on the car radio, and I hope they will smile, as I smile, at the tale of how, on toward the seventh inning stretch, our father would take a flashlight and walk over to the creek, reach in under the old corduroy bridge and come up with a handful of wild beer.

This is the Ottawa Valley of their grandfather and grandmother, the Ottawa Valley of their father and uncles and aunt, who did not get to know it as well as their parents, the Ottawa Valley of their cousins and their friends and, yes, of Earl, who is now living happily — his eyes still clear, his face unlined — at a senior citizens' home not far from where he spent a lifetime caring for the garden and the young children who would come to visit and play.

Twenty years ago we came back from that drive and the women had all gone indoors. There were bees in the garden and a swallow dipping over the pail of water that would soon hurry on the next round of raspberries. Earl hopped out and hurried over to the porch, suddenly stopping on the top step to turn with that magical, mischievous grin.

"Well," he said, "I wonder who lives here?"

We all do, Earl, we all do.

96

A leap into summer, Mount St. Patrick.

The beauty of old iron, Spencerville.

100

Chickens and shovel, Dacre.

101

Hens in a crate, Almonte.

*Where they say miracles take place. The Holy Well,
Mount St. Patrick.*

Interior of the Holy Well,
Mount St. Patrick.

105

Summer afternoon, Dwyer Hill.

Rich contrasts. Landmark in Killaloe Station.

109

Rest and be thankful. Fairgrounds, Quyon.

Comfort station, Fitzroy Harbour.

111

Summer's green engulfs relics of the past. Spencerville.

Waiting for milking time. Gouldhaven Farms, Queen's Line.

HOLSTEIN BREEDER

GOULDHAVEN FARMS
A. & B. GOULD

Broom in barbershop, Richmond.

116

The fairgrounds, Carp.

117

ABOUT THE AUTHORS...

STEVE EVANS

was born in Richmond in the Ottawa Valley in 1955.
He is celebrated for his best-selling photo-documentaries
of the Valley's people: *Heart and Soul* (1987),
Up the Line (1989), and *The Back Forty* (1990), with
Barbara Sibbald. Steve still lives in Richmond, and he is
studying history at Carleton University in Ottawa.

ROY MACGREGOR

was born in the village of Whitney in the Upper Ottawa
Valley in 1948. Winner of more than a dozen national
journalism awards, he is the author of five previous
books, including *The Last Season,* a novel set in the
Valley, and the No. 1 Canadian bestseller of 1989-90,
Home Game, with hockey legend Ken Dryden.
Roy is a daily columnist with The Ottawa Citizen and
lives in Kanata with Ellen and their four children.